Life in the THIRTEEN COLONIES

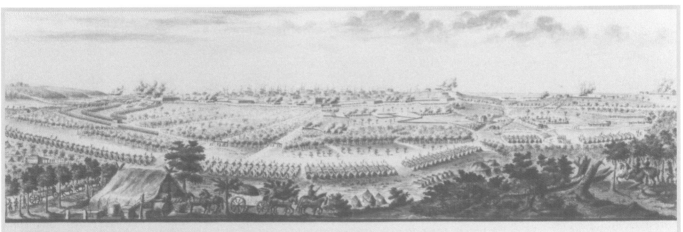

Vue de la Ville de Savannah, du Camp, des Tranchées et de L'attaque Octobre 1779.

Georgia

Robin S. Doak

children's press ®
An imprint of
■ SCHOLASTIC

Library of Congress Cataloging-in-Publication Data

Doak, Robin S. (Robin Santos), 1963–
  Georgia / By Robin S. Doak.
    p. cm. — (Life in the thirteen colonies)
  Includes bibliographical references and index.
  ISBN 0–516–24570–8
  1. Georgia—History—Colonial period, ca. 1600–1775—Juvenile literature. 2. Georgia—History—
1775–1865—Juvenile literature. I. Title. II. Series.
  F289.D63 2004
  975.8'02—dc22
                                    2004010548

1 2 3 4 5 6 7 8 9 10 R 13 12 11 10 09 08 07 06 05 04

A Creative Media Applications Production
Design: Fabia Wargin Design
Editor: Matt Levine
Copy Editor: Laura Lieb
Proofreader: Tania Bissell
Content Research: Lauren Thogersen
Photo Researcher: Annette Cyr
Content Consultant: David Silverman, Ph.D.

CONTENTS

THE
ORIGINAL
THIRTEEN COLONIES,
1775

NEW FRANCE

MAINE
(part of Mass.)

St. Lawrence River

Lake Champlain

NEW HAMPSHIRE

Connecticut River

Falmouth

Portsmouth
Newburyport

Lake Ontario

Mohawk R.

Albany

NEW YORK

Salem
Boston

MASSACHUSETTS

Cape Cod

Hartford

Lake Erie

Hudson R.

New Haven

Newport

RHODE ISLAND
CONNECTICUT

Delaware R.

Susquehanna R.

New York

Long Island

Perth Amboy

PENNSYLVANIA

Philadelphia

Burlington

Pittsburgh

York

New Castle

NEW JERSEY

Ohio River

Potomac R.

Baltimore

MARYLAND

DELAWARE

Alexandria

Atlantic Ocean

Chesapeake Bay

James River

Richmond

Williamsburg

VIRGINIA

Norfolk

Roanoke River

Edenton

Hillsboro

Halifax

Cape Hatteras

Salem

NORTH CAROLINA

Bath

Salisbury

New Bern

Charlotte

Pamlico Sound

Cross Creek

Cape Fear R.

Wilmington

Camden

SOUTH CAROLINA

Georgetown

Savannah River

Augusta

Charles Town

GEORGIA

Savannah

SPANISH TERRITORY

NORTH

EAST

WEST

SOUTH

Legend

Colonial boundaries
(The western boundaries of many colonies were undefined in 1775.)

0   125   250

Scale in Miles

A Nation Grows
From Thirteen Colonies

Georgia lies in the southeastern region of the United States of America. Its eastern border is the Atlantic Ocean. South Carolina lies to the north. Alabama borders Georgia to the west. Florida lies to the south.

Indians called Georgia home for thousands of years before the first Europeans arrived. As more and more settlers came to Georgia, the Indians were pushed from their lands. These settlers brought African slaves to the colony and established large plantations based on slave labor. In addition, small farmers and merchants helped the colony grow.

Georgia would become a key battleground during the war that the colonies fought for independence. It was the thirteenth state to sign the Declaration of Independence and the fourth state to ratify the U.S. Constitution.

The map shows the thirteen English colonies in 1775. The colored sections show the areas that were settled at that time.

CHAPTER ONE

Discovery

Georgia was the most southern of the original thirteen colonies. Founded in 1733, it was also the last to be settled. Massachusetts, the first original colony, had existed for more than 100 years by the time English settlers began colonizing Georgia.

But even before it was colonized by Europeans, people lived on the land that would become Georgia. The earliest Native American people moved into the area 11,000 years ago. These people were nomads, or wanderers. They hunted deer and turkey and gathered nuts and plants in order to survive.

Between A.D. 800 and 1600, people known as the Mound Builders lived in the Georgia region. They were called Mound Builders because they created large hills of dirt in their villages. They built homes on top of these mounds and held religious ceremonies there. Some of the these mounds were burial sites.

Many Native Americans of Georgia lived in fenced villages. Their huts surrounded a council house where meetings and celebrations took place.

The Mound Builders are thought to be the ancestors of the Creek Indians. By the mid-1500s, the Creek and the Cherokee were the most powerful Native American tribes in the area. The Creek were the larger of the two tribes. They were, in fact, a combination of tribes that had banded together for peace. The tribes were stronger and safer together than they were apart.

English traders called the combined tribes the Creek because many lived along the Ochese Creek, near what is now Macon. The Creek Confederacy (union) included such tribes as the Creek, the Yamasee, and the Oconi. These tribes shared the same language, Muskogean.

The Creek

Creek tribes lived in settled villages called *italwa*. The heart of each village was a large open area called the *pascova*. Here, tribal members held ceremonies, danced, and played games. Important tribal meetings also took place in the *pascova*.

Each village was ruled by a chief called a *mico*. A *mico* who did well was allowed to continue ruling by the tribe. Tribal members could replace a bad *mico* with someone else.

The doctor was also important. The Creek doctor treated snake bites, insect stings, diarrhea, colds, and other illnesses. He used leaves, herbs, and roots to make medicines. The tribal doctor often sang or chanted while making medicines.

Creek homes were huts made of wood and mud. They were roofed with grass, straw, or **shingles.** Later, around the time the British settled in the area, the Creek began building log homes in the style of colonists to the north.

The Creek were farmers. Inside their fenced villages, tribes grew rice, corn, potatoes, and other crops. The Creek also raised such livestock as cattle and pigs.

The Green Corn Festival

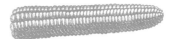

The Green Corn Festival was an annual festival and religious celebration held by both the Creek and Cherokee people. It was held each year when the first ears of corn were ready to harvest. During one part of the festival, tribe members fasted and drank an herbal mixture called the "Black Drink" to clean out the body. Then they gathered at the *pascova* to light the sacred fire. The ears of corn were boiled and hung around the *pascova* as an offering to the Great Spirit. Later, the entire village danced, sang, and feasted on a variety of corn dishes to celebrate the beginning of harvest season.

The Cherokee

The other powerful tribe in the region, the Cherokee, began settling Georgia in the 1450s. The tribe had been forced south after unsuccessful wars with other native tribes. In the 1600s, the Cherokee began to take over parts of Georgia. As they did so, they forced Creek tribes further south.

Like the Creek, the Cherokee were a farming people. They grew corn, squash, beans, and other crops. Cherokee women gathered berries, roots, and other edible plants. Cherokee men hunted for deer to help feed the family.

The Cherokee lived in permanent villages of thirty to sixty houses. These homes were made out of branches woven together to form circular shapes. The spaces between the branches were then filled in with clay and twigs.

Cherokee Indian homes were made of large branches woven in a circular shape. The spaces between the branches were then filled in with clay and twigs to keep out the wind and rain.

The center of each village was a large council house. The council house was used for meetings and religious ceremonies. A sacred fire was kept burning there at all times.

The Creek and Cherokee were hardworking, but they also found time for fun. They enjoyed music, dancing, and games. Men and women both played a game similar to lacrosse. Players held wooden sticks. One end of each stick was carved into a cup or had a woven net attached. The players used the sticks to carry and throw a small animal-hide ball at a cow skull on a wooden post.

The two tribes played different versions of this stick game, which was known as *toli*. The Cherokee version was rougher. Players could tackle one another to prevent their opponents from scoring. Sometimes, the Creek and Cherokee even used stickball matches to settle disputes. These contests could last all day long.

Unlike the Creek, the Cherokee spoke Iroquoian. The name *Cherokee* comes from the Creek word *chelokee*, which means "people of a different speech."

First Contacts

In the early 1500s, Europeans began visiting what is now Georgia. The first people to explore the coast of Georgia were from Spain. In 1521, Spanish slave ships sailed to the coast of Georgia from Spain's colonies in the Caribbean.

The Spanish were looking for new sources of Indian slaves to work on their plantations on the islands. They kidnapped some Yamasee people in Georgia.

Five years later, Spain decided to establish a colony in Georgia. The new settlement, founded somewhere along Georgia's coast, was a miserable failure. It was attacked by natives who did not want to be enslaved by the newcomers. Slaves living in the settlement also rebelled against Spanish rule. The Spanish abandoned the settlement after just six weeks.

In the decades that followed, the Spanish continued to explore much of the Georgia region. One of the largest expeditions into the area began in 1539. That year, Hernando de Soto led an army of 600 soldiers through Florida and into southwestern Georgia. De Soto, a Spanish conquistador, or conqueror, was in search of gold and jewels. He and his men followed Native American trails through the southeast.

De Soto visited many native villages during his long journey. His visits were not pleasant for the Indians. In one village, located near what is now Rome, de Soto arrested tribal leaders. He forced other tribe members to go with him as slaves. Before he left, he took the grain that the villagers had stored for the winter. De Soto left little behind to help the natives survive the winter.

When de Soto left the region, he and his men may have left behind such diseases as smallpox and the plague. These diseases did not exist in North America. They took a deadly toll on the native people in the area. Because the natives had no natural defenses against these diseases, they were at high risk for illness. As a result, the population of the tribes in the area began to **decline**. In some parts of Georgia, the native population **plummeted** by 90 percent.

Spanish explorers like Hernando de Soto were cruel to the Native Americans of Georgia. The Spanish captured and enslaved many tribe members.

Spanish Missions

Nearly seventy years after the first failed Spanish settlement, the first successful Spanish mission in Georgia was founded by Catholic priests on Cumberland Island. The missionaries hoped to convert the Native Americans of the region to Christianity. Other early missions were founded along Georgia's coast.

Relations between missionaries and natives were not always friendly. In 1597, for example, several priests were killed in a native rebellion. Shortly afterward, a number of missions along the coast were closed as native populations in the region declined from disease. The last Spanish coastal mission was destroyed by pirates from South Carolina in 1684. The last mission further inland was destroyed by the Creek Indians in 1706.

The Spanish were not the only Europeans to come in contact with the native tribes. North of Georgia, the British had founded South Carolina. The British colonists would also affect the lives of Georgia's native people.

Contact with the Europeans caused problems for the Cherokee. Between 1729 and 1753, smallpox **epidemics** swept through the tribe. According to some estimates, the tribal population was cut in half as a result.

Georgia Pirates

Before British colonists settled in Georgia, pirates often used the area's coastal islands, rivers, and swamps as hiding places. One of the most infamous pirates to seek shelter along Georgia's coast was Captain Edward Teach. He was better known as Blackbeard. Blackbeard began his career in the early 1700s. The British hired him to attack enemy Spanish ships loaded with gold. Blackbeard turned to piracy when Spain and Britain made peace.

The pirate and his ship, *Queen Anne's Revenge,* terrified anyone who had the bad fortune to see them. Blackbeard was said to be tall, with black hair and a black beard wound into small braids and decorated with ribbons. When he attacked a ship, he would place slow-burning pieces of rope in his hair and beard. The smoking rope made Blackbeard look like he was on fire. This would terrify the enemy crew.

Blackbeard was killed in a sword fight with British lieutenant Robert Maynard.

In November 1718, Blackbeard was killed while battling aboard a British ship. Before his death, the pirate told others that he had hidden his treasure where only he and the devil could find it. Today, treasure hunters still seek the pirate's riches on some of Georgia's coastal islands. So far, no pirate booty has been found.

Appalachian Mountains

Rome

Broad River

Heard's Fort ◇

Augusta •

Savannah River

SOUTH
CAROLINA

NORTH

WEST   EAST

SOUTH

Macon •

Oconee River

Ogeechee River

GEORGIA

Ocmulgee River

Fort
Moore

Savannah •

Tybee
Island

Yamacraw
Bluff

Altamaha River

Darien •

◇ Fort Frederica

Satilla River

St. Marys River

Cumberland
Island

Atlantic
Ocean

GEORGIA,
1775

SPANISH TERRITORY

Legend

——— Colonial boundaries
(The western boundaries of many
colonies were undefined in 1775.)

0   25   50
Scale in Miles

CHAPTER TWO

A Noble Experiment

❦❦❦❦❦❦❦❦❦❦❦❦❦❦❦❦❦❦❦❦❦❦❦❦❦❦❦❦❦❦❦❦

British Traders

Beginning in 1674, British colonists from South Carolina began visiting the Georgia area. Many of these early explorers were traders, looking for deerskins and slaves. Over the years, an important trading business developed between the native people in Georgia and the South Carolina colonists.

The chief product that the Creek and Cherokee traded was deerskins. The skins were shipped back to England. There, they were made into pants, gloves, and other items. Both tribes also supplied slaves from enemy tribes to the British colonists. In exchange for deerskins and slaves, the tribes received cloth, weapons, and rum.

This map shows how Georgia looked in 1775.

Native people in Georgia hunted deer and other wildlife. They traded the animal skins to British colonists.

By the early 1700s, the unsettled region that would soon be known as Georgia was sandwiched between two enemies, Spain and Great Britain. Spanish settlements in Florida bordered Georgia to the south. To the north lay

South Carolina and the rest of England's colonies. Both empires believed that they had a strong claim to Georgia. Even though there were no Spanish missions left in the region, Spain still viewed the area as its own. Before long, violence between the two nations would erupt.

Georgia Beginnings

On January 14, 1733, the British ship *Anne* arrived off the coast of the South Carolina colony. On board were General James Edward Oglethorpe and 114 English settlers. They hoped to start a new colony.

One week later, Oglethorpe and several others sailed up the Savannah River. They were searching for a good spot to build the first settlement in the colony that he had named Georgia, after King George II. This river formed the border between Georgia and South Carolina.

Oglethorpe chose a high cliff near the mouth of the Savannah River. The cliff was known as Yamacraw **Bluff**. It was located just 16 miles (256 kilometers) inland from the Atlantic Ocean. Oglethorpe reasoned that the high site would be the perfect spot for a new settlement. It would be safe from river flooding. It would also be easy to defend from enemies.

The Great Experiment

For years, Oglethorpe had dreamed of founding a new colony in North America. He wanted to create a home for poor people and those who were not allowed to practice their religion in England. In his *Rationale for Founding the Georgia Colony*, Oglethorpe laid out his reasons for creating such a place. "By such a Colony," he wrote, "many families, who would otherwise starve, will be provided for, and made masters of houses and lands."

James Oglethorpe had firsthand knowledge of how England's poor were treated. A close friend died from neglect while serving time in a special type of jail for people who owed money, called debtor's prison. Oglethorpe wanted to make sure that this did not happen to other poor people.

Nine months before he sailed up the Savannah River, Oglethorpe received a twenty-one-year **charter** from King George II of England. The charter allowed Oglethorpe and twenty other men, called **trustees,** to set up a thirteenth British colony in the area between the Savannah and Altamaha rivers. A trustee is a person who safeguards the property and affairs of a company or another person. The trustees would manage the new colony from England. Only Oglethorpe would travel to Georgia, as "resident trustee."

Although the trustees intended Georgia to be an experiment in fairness and tolerance, King George had more practical plans for the colony. The king needed a **buffer** colony, a settlement that would separate his colonies to the north from their Spanish enemies in Florida. He also wanted to make sure that the world knew about England's claim to the area below South Carolina. Finally, he hoped that the newest colony would produce silk and other goods to be shipped back to England. For this reason, silkworms and white mulberry trees were sent to Georgia. The leaves of the tree are a favorite food of the silk-making insects.

James Oglethorpe traveled to Georgia and met with the Indians who lived there.

After the king granted the trustees their charter, the search for suitable colonists began. People who applied to travel to Georgia had to go through a long selection process. Each colonist had to be interviewed and investigated before he or she was chosen. Oglethorpe selected only those he thought were hardworking, came from good families, and had some education.

To help Georgia survive, **Parliament,** England's law-making body, agreed to send a yearly payment to the colony. Georgia was the only British colony that ever received such a payment. The colony would need these funds, because its first few years would prove to be rocky ones.

Welcome to Savannah

The Savannah settlement was to be located on a 40-foot-high (12-meter) bluff. The first thing that needed to be built there was a set of wooden steps leading up from the river. On February 12, 1733, the first settlers climbed these steps to the site of their new home. Today, that date is celebrated each year as Georgia's birthday.

Next, shelter was needed to protect the new colonists from the cold and rain. Before houses were built, the 114 settlers lived in five big tents. Oglethorpe had a smaller tent all to himself.

Oglethorpe and Colonel William Bull of South Carolina quickly began mapping out the settlement of Savannah. Together, they planned a community. They divided the settlement into square plots of land. Each square with the area around it was called a **ward.** Savannah was the first planned city in America.

Early Savannah consisted of four wards. Over time, however, the town would grow and prosper. Eventually, it would expand to include twenty-four wards. Today, twenty-one of the original twenty-four squares still exist in Savannah.

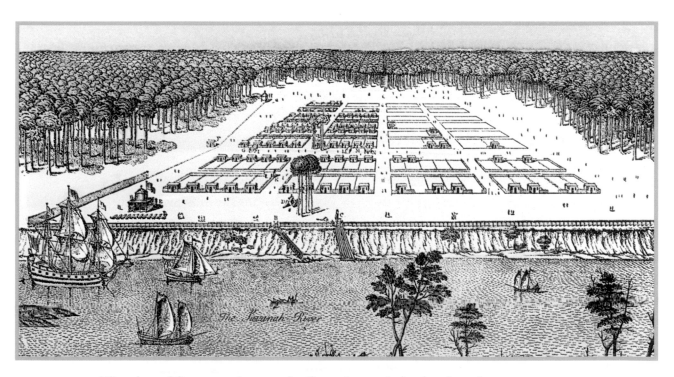

The city of Savannah was the first planned city in America.

The first structure to be built was a **palisade**, or fence, to protect the new settlement. Later, five cannons would be shipped to Savannah to defend the town. Once the fence was finished, settlers could begin constructing their homes. A large, hand-cranked crane was used to lift wood and other materials to the top of the bluff.

At this time, large mansions were being built by wealthy people in other colonies. Compared to these, Savannah's first homes were quite humble. They were small cabins with clay walls. A fireplace was used for cooking, as well as heating on damp winter days.

Keeping Clean, Colonial Style

In the new colony, keeping clean was often a difficult task. For early Georgians, washing up usually meant cleaning off the hands and face. A colonial home might include a washbasin and pitcher for this purpose. When colonists needed a complete bath, they took a dip in a wooden tub. Sometimes, the water was heated before the bath. At other times, the water was cold. Most people in Georgia and other colonies avoided taking such baths more than once or twice a year. In the eighteenth century, many people believed that bathing was likely to make a person sick.

To avoid smelling the foul odors all around them, colonists sometimes carried pieces of cloth dipped in perfume. Such a scented cloth was held to the nose when the other smells became too strong.

Savannah's Colonists

For the first year, the colonists worked together to make sure their settlement was a success. At the end of the year, each adult male received a 50-acre (20-hectare) parcel of land. Five of these acres included a building and garden lot within Savannah itself. The other 45 acres (18 hectares) were outside the settlement. These acres were used for crops and livestock. In addition to land, settlers were also given livestock, seeds for planting, and farming equipment.

Although the colony had been founded as a haven for the poor, wealthy people were also encouraged to settle in Georgia. Wealthy settlers who brought servants to the colony were given larger parcels of land. The trustees thought that these servants would help the new colony grow and prosper. People coming to Georgia were allowed to bring as many as ten servants with them. Those who brought ten servants were given 500 acres (200 hectares). This was the maximum amount allowed.

People who traveled to Georgia as servants came as indentured servants. This meant that their masters agreed to pay for their passage to Georgia. In exchange, the servants agreed to work for a given period of time. This period was usually five to seven years but could be as long as fourteen years. Once the servants had finished their period of service, they were given their own pieces of land.

Indentured servants in Georgia sometimes learned useful trades. When their time of service was up, they could use their new skills to make a good living in the colony.

Indentured servitude was not very successful in Georgia. Many servants, once in the colonies, ran away to South Carolina. There, the runaways found a successful economy. In South Carolina, there were many economic opportunities that were not available in the struggling thirteenth colony.

Savannah grew slowly. By 1740, the settlement was home to a jail, a courthouse, a warehouse, and a **wharf.** According to *A State of the Province of Georgia*, a pamphlet published in 1740, Savannah also had a "large house for receiving the Indians" and a public garden. The beautiful 10-acre (4-hectare) garden had many fruit trees. There were also olive trees, mulberry trees, and plants that could be used to make medicines.

Struggling for Survival

For many colonists, adapting to life in Savannah was difficult. The settlers from England were not used to the swampy, humid climate. Fresh water was scarce, insects were plentiful, and alligators lurked in the river. During the town's early years, many of the original settlers died of illness.

The colony also lacked the strong political structure that held other colonies together. Other than Oglethorpe and the trustees, there was no government in the colony. However, there were rules. Georgia's earliest rules were written by the trustees. Under the rules, rum and hard liquor were banned from the colony. The trustees believed that drinking would only cause laziness and other problems. Slavery was also banned, making Georgia the only colony to prohibit this practice.

Some colonists were able to prosper by raising cattle or taking part in the fur trade. But most of Georgia's early colonists struggled to survive. Some of the settlers were at a  disadvantage right from the start. Many were from London (England's capital) and other cities. They knew nothing about farming. But other settlers did understand farming. These people soon realized that much of the land around Savannah was not fertile enough to support everyone in the colony.

Despite the difficulties of life in early Georgia, people from other European countries migrated to the colony. Many were attracted to Georgia by the promise of religious freedom. Some of the new arrivals were assigned chunks of land outside of Savannah. Others founded their own towns, including Ebenezer and Darien.

One early Georgia town was Augusta. This town was located upriver from Savannah. The town began as a Carolina trading post called Fort Moore. By 1740, the little settlement, renamed Augusta, had become a center of frontier trade. The river trip between Augusta and Savannah could take between three and four weeks, depending upon the currents.

Native Americans and Early Settlers

Oglethorpe knew that his colony would have a better chance of survival if relations with the native people of the region were good. When he first arrived in Georgia, he asked permission from local tribes to settle in the area. He also promised to make sure that traders from Carolina treated the tribes fairly.

James Oglethorpe knew that the success of his colony depended, in part, on friendship with the Indians.

Oglethorpe's efforts paid off. The Creek Indians helped the first settlers in Savannah survive their early years. They supplied the settlers with food and gave them information about the Georgia area and the other native groups who lived there.

One of the most important native figures during Georgia's early days was the Yamacraw chief Tomochichi. The Yamacraw were a tribe made up of Creek and Yamasee people. Tomochichi encouraged peaceful relations between his tribe and the new arrivals. He also convinced other tribes to befriend the English settlers. Tomochichi died in 1739. Oglethorpe honored his native friend with a military funeral and a special grave marker in Savannah.

Another native who was important to the early settlers was Mary Musgrove. She was known as Coosaponakeesa by the Creek Indians. Musgrove's husband was a white trader from South Carolina. They owned a trading post on Yamacraw Bluff. When Oglethorpe arrived in the area, Musgrove served as his interpreter with the Creek. After her husband's death, she opened a new trading post, called Cowpens. This trading post served as an important source of food and other supplies for the colonists.

The Public Midwife

The public midwife was the only paid government position for a woman in Georgia. The midwife visited pregnant women and helped them deliver their babies safely. In a time when few doctors and no hospitals existed in Georgia, the public midwife was a very important person. The first midwife was hired by the trustees to care for women in Savannah. Later, midwives were hired to care for women in the northern and southern regions of the colony. The public midwife was paid about £5 each year, equal to about $885 in today's dollars. Part of the midwife's pay was an allowance for wine to ease the pain of women in labor.

Women in Early Georgia

The first female settlers in Georgia played a key role in helping the new colony survive. The trustees encouraged families to settle in Georgia. They believed that single men were "very great inconveniences."

A woman's role in Georgia was to be "a loving Wife, an affectionate Mother, and a true Housekeeper." Women were expected to carry out traditional female tasks. These included caring for and teaching their children, cooking and preserving food, and keeping the home clean. They also performed much other work that needed to be done, such as chopping wood, plowing, planting, and picking crops. In addition, some women in early Georgia owned or operated taverns and inns.

Women in Georgia worked as hard as the men. They were not, however, given the same rights as men. They could not own land. They could not be left land when husbands or fathers died. If a Georgia landowner died without any male heirs, his land went back to the trustees. It was not long before men and women alike began to protest this unfair policy. Eventually, the trustees began allowing widows and female children to inherit land.

Children in Georgia

Colonial children were expected to help out in the new colony. Once children reached the age of six, they were given chores to complete. Young girls were taught how to cook, clean, and sew. They learned how to spin and dye cloth, and care for the family's livestock. Young boys were taught to care for the livestock. They also had to pick vegetables from the garden, chop wood, and help their fathers in the fields.

Children were allowed to play games with their brothers and sisters only when all their chores had been completed.

Play Time in Georgia

Just like children today, colonial children loved to play. Of course, there were no big toy stores stocked with the latest toys. Instead, colonial toys were usually homemade. For example, girls made dolls out of cornhusks and bits of cloth. Boys made playhouses out of corncobs.

In colonial times, large families were common. The largest of families might have more than a dozen children. As a result, children usually had plenty of playmates. They might play popular games of the time or make up their own. One favorite game was scotch hoppers, known today as hopscotch. Colonial children also played many different types of tag.

In general, colonial children were meant to be seen and not heard. They were expected to obey their parents and not complain. They usually ate their meals in silence. In some families, children were not allowed to sit at the table. Instead, they stood behind the adults and had their meals handed back to them.

The type of education that a child in Georgia received depended on whether the child was a boy or girl. It was believed that learning from books was more important for boys than for girls. As a result, boys were taught reading, writing, and other skills that they would need to make a living. Girls might learn reading and writing, but they were also taught such "feminine" skills as needlepoint and dancing.

At first, most children were taught at home by their own parents. As the colony grew, neighbors might get together and hire a tutor for all their children, or one parent might serve as a teacher to the area children. A small school building was usually built in an old field that was not good for growing crops. As a result, the schools came to be known as old-field schools. There were few books and other supplies in these old-field schools. Children often traced their letters and numbers in the dust or in ashes. School attendance was spotty. Children did not go to school if they had to help out at home or on the farm.

Bethesda, America's Oldest Orphanage

In March 1740, George Whitefield began building an orphanage 10 miles (16 kilometers) from Savannah. The year before, this Protestant preacher was given a grant of 500 acres (200 hectares) along the Moon River. He hoped to provide shelter and a good education to forty poor boys.

The Bethesda Orphanage had three buildings. The main building, where the boys lived, was a two-story house with twenty-one rooms. The two smaller buildings were a work-house and a hospital. In the workhouse, the children learned skills to help them find work as adults. They were taught spinning, **mechanics**, and farming. The boys also tended the gardens and cared for the livestock. Today, the Bethesda Home for Boys still exists in the same place.

Wealthy parents could choose to send their children to other colonies or back to England to get a good education. Poorer children received less education. Some poor boys were apprenticed to tradesmen at the age of eight. An **apprentice** would be taught the skills needed to do carpentry, blacksmithing, or other important jobs.

Children were considered grown at a younger age than today's children. Colonial girls usually married at the age of sixteen. The family of a young woman who reached the age of eighteen might begin to worry that she would never marry. At the age of sixteen, boys were considered men. They began paying taxes and could join the militia (a group of citizen-soldiers).

CHAPTER THREE

A Struggling Colony

James Oglethorpe had high hopes for his colony. He firmly believed that Georgia could become as prosperous as its sister colonies to the north. Oglethorpe hoped that the colony might someday be able to supply South Carolina with food, silk, timber, and other products.

Despite Oglethorpe's best intentions, his colony did not thrive during its first few years. Georgia had a high death rate. Crops around Savannah did not grow as expected. As the years wore on, problems in the new settlement grew worse.

In addition, Oglethorpe also had to worry about Spanish forces to the south. The Spanish were very unhappy when Oglethorpe began colonizing Georgia. They believed that they had a good claim to the area. Spanish missionaries and explorers had been working in the area for nearly two centuries before Oglethorpe arrived.

🖎 *While Oglethorpe lived in Georgia, he created good relations between the colonists and the native people.*

Problems With Spain

Oglethorpe wanted to protect his new colony from Spanish attacks. He began building forts along Georgia's coastline. The first, built in 1736, was Fort Frederica. Located on Saint Simons Island, the fort served as Oglethorpe's headquarters. Other strongholds were soon built to the south.

In 1739, war broke out between Spain and Great Britain. The conflict, known as the War of Jenkins's Ear, soon affected Georgia. It all started when Robert Jenkins, a British smuggler, was captured by a Spanish military ship. The Spaniards took his cargo and cut off one of his ears to punish him further.

During the War of Jenkins's Ear, Georgia colonists aided British soldiers fighting against Spain.

The war caused relations to worsen between Georgia's colonists and their Spanish neighbors to the south. Oglethorpe and other Georgians worried that the Spanish might try to take control of the colony. So in January 1740, Oglethorpe invaded Florida and captured two Spanish forts. His success made Oglethorpe bold. The general planned an attack on St. Augustine. This settlement served as Spain's headquarters in Florida. Oglethorpe's attack failed.

In 1742, the Battle of Bloody Marsh finally settled the question of who would control Georgia. On July 7, as many as 5,000 Spanish soldiers attacked Fort Frederica. With the help of Native American warriors, Oglethorpe and his men defeated the Spanish. The British victory at Bloody Marsh ended Spanish claims in Georgia. In 1748, Great Britain and Spain signed a treaty to officially make the Saint John River the boundary between Spanish Florida and British Georgia.

Tricking the Enemy

If it was not for the quick thinking of James Oglethorpe at Bloody Marsh, the British might have lost control of Georgia. After the battle, a French spy told the Spanish that Oglethorpe's troops were weak. The spy said that the British could easily be defeated if they were attacked again. Oglethorpe learned about the spy and his activities. He told the spy a false story: British troops were on the way to help. The spy told the Spanish, and they fled.

Life in Frederica

The area around Fort Frederica soon developed into a thriving town called Frederica. Just seven years after the fort was built, about 1,000 colonists were living there. Frederica was made up of two separate sections connected by a central roadway. The road, known as Broad Street, connected the new settlement to the fort. Orange trees were planted on both sides of Broad Street to shade hot and weary travelers.

Oglethorpe divided Frederica into eighty-four lots. Every family who settled there was given one lot, plus an acre outside of town for a garden. Settlers were also given fifty acres farther from town for raising crops.

Building With Tabby

Oglethorpe wanted Fort Frederica to withstand Spanish attacks. He chose to build its walls out of a material called tabby. Tabby is a cement-like substance made out of equal amounts of crushed oyster shells, lime (a substance made by burning rock, shells, and bones), sand, and water. Tabby was inexpensive and very sturdy.

As more people settled along the Georgia coast, they began building their homes with tabby. This material soon came to be known as "coastal concrete." For fancier homes, the surfaces of the tabby walls were covered with stucco, or plaster. Then they were whitewashed, or painted with a mixture of lime and water.

The first settlers in Frederica built temporary homes out of sticks and the large leaves of palmetto trees. These early homes, called palmetto bowers, gave settlers shelter from the sun and the rain. Unlike other settlements founded in Georgia, Frederica was never meant to survive without help from the king of England. The colonists relied on shipments of goods from Great Britain.

Oglethorpe had 5,000 mulberry trees sent to Frederica in the hopes that

The first homes in Frederica were temporary ones. They were made out of sticks and leaves.

the settlers would try silk production. His silk scheme failed, however. After the 1748 treaty between Spain and Great Britain, the fort was no longer needed and the soldiers housed there left. The town quickly declined as settlers followed, moving to other areas. In 1758, a fire destroyed what was left of the town. Any colonists who had remained moved elsewhere.

Problems Within the Colony

Oglethorpe faced serious problems in Georgia. These would prove more dangerous to his dreams than the threat from Spain. By the 1740s, many people in Georgia were unhappy with their quality of life. The economy was suffering, crops were not growing, and settlers were fleeing from the colony. By 1743, only about 500 settlers remained in the newest colony. The general's Great Experiment was on the verge of failing.

The ban on rum was also hurting the colony's economy. Georgia could have traded its timber for rum in the West Indies. The rum could then have been sold in the colonies for other goods. But because importing rum into the colony was banned, trade with the West Indies was effectively shut off.

A Disorganized Colony

Georgia society was not doing well, either. There were no public schools. The delivery of mail from other colonies was not reliable. The only roads in the colony were the narrow trails used by the natives. People traveled on these paths on foot or on horseback. The only town of any importance at all was Savannah.

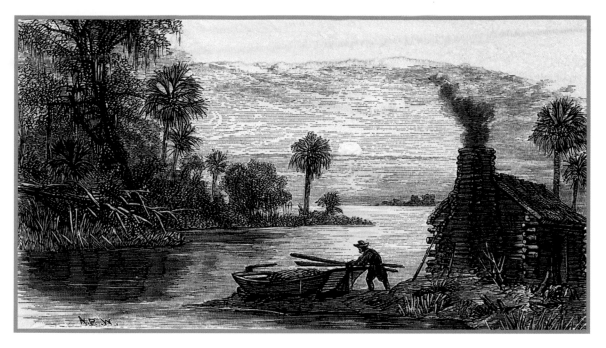

Many early settlers lived far from Savannah, the colony's only prosperous city.

Georgia also suffered from the lack of an effective government. The trustees made all the major decisions for the colony, and the trustees were all back in England (except Oglethorpe). The colonists could not vote. They had little or no say in what the trustees did. The only real government in Savannah was a court with three judges, a recorder (a person who wrote and kept the town's records), and a few constables (local police officers). This government was effective only in and around Savannah. Those who settled far away had to create their own systems of order and control.

The Malcontents

People who were unhappy with the trustee system banded together. This group came to be called the malcontents. A malcontent is a person who is not happy with the government. The malcontents in Georgia were made up mainly of Scottish settlers. They opposed many of the rules that the trustees had passed.

During the colony's early years, the malcontents wrote letters and pamphlets complaining about the trustees. These writings said that the trustees' laws were keeping Georgia from growing. In one pamphlet, the group listed twelve reasons why Georgia was failing. They described their colony with these words: "The poor Inhabitants of Georgia are scatter'd over the Face of the Earth; her Plantation a Wild; her Towns a Desert; her Villages in Rubbish…an Object of Pity to Friends, and of Insult, Contempt and Ridicule to Enemies."

The malcontents believed that in order for Georgia to grow, the ban on slavery must be lifted. These colonists saw South Carolina's booming economy, and they wanted the same for Georgia. They wanted a plantation economy, and this meant slaves. A plantation economy relies on large farms to make money and large numbers of slaves to do the work on the plantations.

The malcontents became more outspoken. Around the same time, Oglethorpe was losing interest in Georgia. He knew that his colony was not doing well. Oglethorpe blamed the failure, in part, on the trustees back in England. He had expected more support from them, in the form of money and goods. In 1743, Oglethorpe was called back to England. He never returned to the colony he had founded.

A Malcontent Complaint

At the end of December 1738, a group of Georgia colonists sent a petition, or written request, to the trustees. The colonists asked for ownership of their lands without any conditions. They also asked that the ban on slavery be lifted. The petition included the following comparison to their neighbor to the north, slave-holding South Carolina: "It is very well known, that Carolina can raise every thing that this Colony can; and they having their Labour so much cheaper will always ruin our Market, unless we are in some Measure on a Footing with them." The petition also included a threat. "If, by denying us these Privileges, we ourselves and Families are not only ruin'd...You will always be mentioned as the Cause and Authors of all their Misfortunes and Calamities; which we hope will never happen."

The complaints of the malcontents were successful. In 1750, the trustees lifted the ban on slavery.

CHAPTER FOUR

A Royal Colony

No More Trustees

In 1751, Georgia's colonists took the first step toward self-government. That year, the first colonial assembly, or lawmaking body, met in Savannah. The assembly was made up of representatives from the various towns, settlements, and large families in Georgia.

The representatives had no power to pass laws. However, they were able to suggest improvements for the colony. These suggestions were then sent to the trustees in London. The representatives first suggested that Georgia be given a new colonial charter. They also asked for the power to make their own laws.

Shortly after the assembly met, the trustees asked Great Britain for more money to support the struggling colony. But Great Britain decided not to send any funds.

🔖 *In 1750, the colony of Georgia was home to about 500 slaves. That number would skyrocket in the coming years.*

Without any money, the trustees knew that their colony would fall apart. In June 1752, they returned control of the colony to the British king and surrendered their charter. This made the British government, not the trustees, responsible for the colony.

With the trustees out of the picture, many colonists became worried. Some believed that South Carolina would try to take control of Georgia. To prevent this, Georgia's colonists wrote to Parliament and the king. They asked that Georgia be made a royal colony, completely separate from South Carolina.

In 1754, Parliament named Georgia a royal colony. This meant that Georgia was now completely under the control of Great Britain. King George sent John Reynolds to serve as the colony's first royal governor. Reynolds arrived in Georgia in October 1754. The colonists were happy to see him.

A New Type of Government

In addition to a royal governor, the colony also gained a lawmaking body called the General Assembly. The first General Assembly, elected in 1754, was divided into two sections. The Upper House was also called the Royal Council. This was a group of twelve men selected by the king. The Lower House was also known as the Commons

House of Assembly. This house was a group of nineteen men elected by the people of Georgia.

The government of the colony was not open to everyone. In order to vote, a colonist had to be a male landowner. To run for a seat in the Lower House, a colonist had to be a male who owned 500 acres (200 hectares). In this way, the running of the colony was confined to the wealthiest of Georgia's colonists.

Before 1754, merchants were not allowed to vote because they did not own land.

Most colonists qualified to vote. But merchants in towns like Savannah and Augusta were unhappy. Because they did not own land, they were not permitted to vote. So Georgia's laws were changed to allow merchants to vote and hold office, as long as they paid a certain amount in taxes.

Governor Reynolds was not able to solve Georgia's problems. He had spent his life as an officer in the navy and was not prepared to govern a colony. After just three years, Reynolds was replaced by Henry Ellis. Under Ellis, the colony was divided into eight districts called parishes. Each parish was required to have a church. Illness forced Ellis to leave Georgia after just three years.

The Start of a Plantation Economy

After becoming a royal colony, Georgia began to slowly expand in size and in population. The colony's borders grew after 1763. The colony's southern border was now set at the Saint Mary's River. The western boundary was set at the Mississippi River. In 1763 and 1773, Georgia's third royal governor, James Wright, signed treaties with the Creek and Cherokee to add even more land to Georgia.

Wright took control of a colony whose economy was in serious trouble. Born in America, Wright had served as South Carolina's attorney general for fifteen years. He was one of the wealthiest plantation owners in South Carolina when he was appointed governor of Georgia. He would quickly become the colony's most popular and successful royal governor.

Shortly before Georgia became a royal colony, the trustees lifted the ban on slavery. Planters from South Carolina, looking for new opportunities, began moving to Georgia. They brought their slaves and the plantation system with them.

Around the time Wright took office, slave traders began bringing slaves from Africa and the West Indies directly into Georgia. Over the next four decades, the colony's slave population would skyrocket from 1,000 to nearly 30,000. In a few years, a small group of planters owned about half the slaves in the colony.

Agriculture, or farming, along the Atlantic coast soon became the mainstay of Georgia's economy.

Georgia planters depended upon slaves to work in the fields.

Growing Rice

The most important crop was rice. Rice was a time-consuming crop to grow. It grew best in the swampy areas along Georgia's coastal rivers. First, swampy coastal areas had to be drained of saltwater. Dikes, which are banks or dams made out of earth to prevent flooding, were then built to keep the saltwater out of the fields. Saltwater could ruin a field, preventing rice from growing for many years to come. Next, a system of canals was built. The canals allowed freshwater to be let into and out of the rice fields as needed.

Growing rice was a year-round activity. In January and February, oxen were used to plow the rice fields. From March through May, the rice was planted in flooded fields. Afterward, the fields were drained, flooded, and drained again until the rice ripened.

In the fall, the rice was harvested and stored in barns. During November and December, the rice was prepared for market. The cut rice plant was banged against a screen or other hard object to separate the grains from the rest of the plant. This process is known as threshing. By 1768, the colony was **exporting** nearly 17,800 barrels of rice a year.

GEORGIA.

By His Excellency Sir *JAMES WRIGHT*, Baronet, Captain-General, Governor, and Commander in Chief, of His Majesty's said Province, Chancellor, Vice-Admiral, and Ordinary of the same,

A PROCLAMATION.

WHEREAS, in obedience to his Majesty's Royal Instructions, a Congress was held at *Augusta* by his said Excellency and the Honourable *John Stuart*, Esquire, his Majesty's Agent and Superintendant of *Indian* Affairs for the Southern District, and sundry Kings, Head-Men, and Warriours, of the *Creek* and *Cherokee Indians*, who were fully authorised and empowered to attend at the said Congress, and to act for their several Nations and Tribes respectively: AND WHEREAS the said *Creek* and *Cherokee Indians* did, at the said Congress, on the first day of this instant *June*, duly make and execute a treaty or deed of cession of certain lands above *Little* River and *Broad* River, upon *Savannah* River, and cross the country towards the *Oconee* River; and also of certain other lands between the *Alatamaha* River and *Ogechee* River; and which lands, by his Majesty's instructions, are to be sold and disposed of to such of his good subjects who may remove into this province to purchase and settle thereon: IT IS THEREFORE HEREBY NOTIFIED, That Surveyors are appointed, and are now running and marking the outlines of the lands ceded as aforesaid, and that the same will be parcelled out in different tracts, as soon as conveniently may be, from 100 to 1000 acres, the better to accommodate the buyers, according to their number in family, and which lands will be sold and granted to the purchasers agreeable to his Majesty's instructions; that is to say, 100 acres to the master or head of the family, and 50 acres for the wife and each child, and also 50 acres for each slave: And, for the further encouragement of the settling of the said lands, the masters or heads of families will be allowed to purchase 50 acres for each able bodied white servant man who they shall bring in to settle thereon, provided such servants be indented for a term not less than two years, to commence from the time they come into the province; and also 25 acres for every woman servant from the age of 15 years to 40 years, provided such women servants be indented for a term not less than two years, to commence from the time they come into the province; and that the master makes oath that such servant or servants are *bona fide* meant to be employed on the said lands, and shall not with his privity or consent remove out of this province during the term of his or her servitude.

AND IT IS FURTHER NOTIFIED, That all persons are now at liberty to come into this province to view the said lands, and, when the surveys are made, then to make choice for themselves of such tract of land as they may like best to purchase and settle upon, and which will be granted them on the most moderate terms according to the quality of the same. AND IT IS FURTHER NOTIFIED, That his most gracious Majesty, as an encouragement to his good subjects to purchase and settle on the said lands, hath been pleased to authorise the Governor of the said province to sign grants exempted from the payment of quit-rents for the term of ten years from the date thereof; and it is also expected that some other exemptions and privileges will be granted to the said settlers by the Legislature of this province. AND IT IS NECESSARY ALSO TO DECLARE, for the information and satisfaction of such as may be disposed to purchase and settle as aforesaid, That the said lands are in general of the most fertile quality, and fit for the production of wheat, *Indian* corn, indico, tobacco, hemp, flax, &c. &c: &c. That it is a pleasant and very healthy part of the province; and that the said lands are extremely well watered by *Savannah* River, O-gechee River, *Little* River, and *Broad* River, and a great number of creeks and branches which run throughout the whole country, and empty themselves into the aforesaid rivers: Also that there is abundance of springs and very fine water: That *Little* River, where the land ceded as aforesaid begins, is but 22 miles above the Town of *Augusta*, which town is only 139 miles above the Town of *Savannah*, which is the seat of government in this province: That the settlers will always find a ready sale and market at *Augusta* for every kind of produce and stock that may be raised by them, or, if they prefer it, have very good and safe water carriage down *Savannah* River to the Town of *Savannah*; and, if they rather choose to carry their produce by land, there is a good waggon-road all the way from *Little* River to *Savannah*. AND IT IS FURTHER NOTIFIED AND DECLARED, That, to the end the said settlers may be safe and secure with respect to their persons and properties, and in order to prevent any interruption to them by disorderly hunters, vagrants, and wanderers, or by any straggling *Indians*, a fort will be forthwith built, and garrisoned by a competent number of Officers and Men to be employed as Rangers for the security and protection of the settlers: That there is a very good and sufficient law in this province for the punishment of vagrants and disorderly white people, and that the several Officers of the Troop of Rangers will be put in the Commission of the Peace, in order the better to enable them to enforce and execute the said law against vagrants, &c. That the said lands adjoin a well settled part of the province, where law, justice, and government, have their full and free force and effect; great blessings to well disposed people, and which cannot be enjoyed in more remote new settlements: And that in general every thing will be done in the power of this province to establish good order in the said settlement, and to promote the interest and happiness of the settlers on the said lands.

Given under my hand and the great seal of his Majesty's said province, in the Council-Chamber at Savannah, the eleventh day of June, in the year of our Lord One thousand seven hundred and seventy-three, and in the thirteenth year of his Majesty's reign.

JA. WRIGHT.

By His Excellency's Command,
THOᵗ. MOODIE, Dep. Secr.

To help Georgia grow, the colony's governors advertised for new colonists.

The Port of Savannah

In the earliest days of the colony, Georgians had relied on the port of Charles Town (now Charleston) in South Carolina for their supplies. But in 1744, Savannah's first merchants had gone into business. From this time on, the shipping of goods into and out of Georgia became an important part of the colony's economy. Soon, trading ships from Savannah were traveling to other colonies, as well as to Europe.

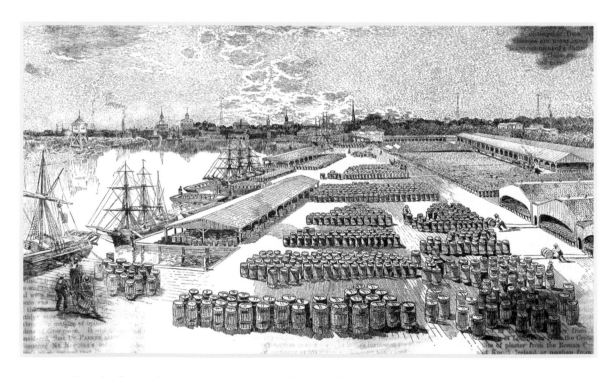

Goods from the other colonies and from Europe were loaded on and off ships at Savannah's busy wharf.

Savannah became even more important after Georgia became a royal colony. Crops such as rice and indigo, a plant used to make blue dye, were shipped out of the port. Georgia's tall pines were cut down and used for lumber. They were made into such naval supplies as oars and masts. These goods, along with deerskins, leather, beef, and pork, were also shipped out of Savannah, the southernmost port in the colonies. Livestock, usually headed for the West Indies, left America from Savannah's port.

Very little manufacturing took place in Georgia. As a result, all manufactured goods were shipped into Savannah from Great Britain and other British colonies. These goods included clothing and furniture, as well as sugar, coffee, and flour. As trade prospered, so did Savannah's merchants. The city soon had warehouses, taverns, coffee shops, and a great variety of stores.

Savannah's High Society

As the colony grew and prospered, the lifestyle of Georgia's richest colonists came to resemble that of South Carolina's plantation owners. Wealthy planters built big brick town houses in Savannah. The planters traveled between Savannah and their plantations in fancy chariots and riding chairs.

Rich plantation owners built huge homes and wore fancy clothes to show off their wealth.

Before long, Savannah had become the cultural center of the colony. Wealthy merchants and lawyers copied the planters' style of living. They, too, built fine mansions surrounded by beautiful gardens.

The fashions of Savannah's richest residents were often imported straight from England. Men and women alike wore garments made of the finest silks and satins. Women wore ankle-length gowns. Men wore short pants called breeches, long fitted vests called waistcoats, and jackets.

Outside the home, women wore their hair up and covered with bonnets or caps. Men wore wigs of many different varieties and styles. These wigs were whitened with chalk dust. Men and women also wore gold and silver jewelry with precious and semiprecious stones.

Unlike people in some of the stricter Protestant colonies, the wealthy of Savannah enjoyed having fun. They took part in dancing, singing, card-playing, horse-racing, and holiday celebrations. However, gambling was banned in Georgia in 1762.

A Georgian Holiday

In colonial times, one of the most festive holidays in Georgia was the celebration of the king's birthday. People drank to the king's health, and British flags flew from every fort and flag-pole. Cannons and rifles were fired throughout the colony in celebration. At night, the colonists gathered at special dinners, bonfires, and other festivities.

Georgians in the Backcountry

Not all of Georgia's new settlers chose to live in Savannah or along the coastal area. Many people decided to create a life in the colony's wild, wooded areas beyond Augusta. This region, known as the backcountry, was Georgia's frontier.

Many of those who made their homes on the frontier were squatters. Squatters are people who settle on land that they do not own. Many of these settlers came from the Carolinas and Virginia.

Life in the backcountry was rough and rugged. Families farmed to survive. They grew vegetables and raised livestock. Some families grew small plots of tobacco. Because the soil was poor, there were no rich planters here. Few families owned slaves.

The backcountry colonists lived close to the native peoples and their lands. They used native trails for hunting and traveling. Some settled on native lands. The Indians were angered by these new arrivals. In the 1760s, groups of Cherokee raided, or attacked and robbed, backcountry settlements. In the winters of 1773 and 1774, Creek Indians also raided homes in the backcountry. These attacks scared off new settlers from the region.

From Creek to Seminole

In the early 1700s, some tribes of Creek Indians migrated from Georgia to uninhabited land in Florida. The Spanish called them *cimarron*, meaning "wild" or "untamed." Eventually, the word *cimmaron* evolved into *Seminole*. Like many Creek, the Seminole supported the British during the war the colonies fought with England to gain their independence.

Seminole Indians, descendants of the Creek, adopted some British practices, including living in log houses.

Georgia's many frontier colonists were also at odds with the wealthy planters who lived in Savannah and along the marshy, coastal lowlands, called the Low Country. They believed that the Low Country men gave special treatment and favors to the colonists around Savannah. In the mid-1700s, this resentment would cause serious problems for the colony. The backcountry settlers would be quicker to join rebel movements against the royal government than other Georgia colonists.

Folk art was produced by some colonists to reflect their traditions and culture. The items were often useful as well as decorative. Some have been passed down from generation to generation since colonial times.

☞ Colonists made drawings of everyday events and used them to decorate their homes. This paper and pencil sketch shows boys rolling hoops, a common colonial game.

Political banners of the time often displayed ⤳ sketches of the people running for office.

The skull decorations on these ☞ gravestones represent the person's soul flying to heaven. ⚑

Here Lyes ye Body of Mary Moore Daughter of Capt Richard & Mrs Mary Moore of Oxford who Decd May ye 27th 1730 Aged 19 Years.

Art

☞ *Skilled colonial woodworkers made musical instruments that were often works of art.*

❦ *Handmade needlepoint samplers like this often decorated colonial homes.*

✎ *Most colonial women and girls were skilled at sewing with fabric. They made rag dolls, rugs from fabric scraps, and beautiful quilts to keep their families warm.*

✐ *Weather vanes placed atop colonial houses were both beautiful and useful.*

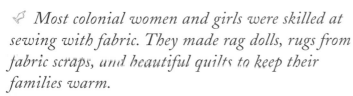

CHAPTER FIVE
Slavery in Georgia

Slave Ships

After the ban on slavery was lifted, Savannah quickly became a major slave port. One of the first slave ships to operate out of Savannah was the *Endeavour*, built in 1747. The *Endeavour* sailed to and from South Carolina, exchanging Georgia goods for slaves.

Slaves were first imported from other colonies and the Caribbean. Later, the majority of slaves were brought directly from West Africa. In Georgia, West African slaves were in high demand because they had knowledge of farming. The first group of slaves directly from Africa arrived on a British ship in 1766.

For slaves, the trip to the American colonies was brutal. The sea voyage, known as the Middle Passage, could take as long as six months. The conditions on board the slave

Savannah was the home port of many slave ships.

ships were horrifying. During the trip, the slaves were treated like animals. In the ship's **hold**, chained Africans were laid side by side on wooden bunks. Sometimes, they were packed so tightly that they had to be chained on their sides. In this position, the head of one slave would be touching the toes of another.

Slaves were treated cruelly during the journey from Africa to the colonies. Many died as a result of the harsh, filthy conditions on slave ships.

Slaves were usually given gruel to eat once a day. In some cases, they were allowed on deck if the weather was good. Vomit, feces, and other body wastes were rinsed off the slaves once every two weeks. These unsanitary conditions took a toll. As many as one out of every four slaves died on the way to America. The sick and dying were dumped into the sea so as not to slow down the voyage.

Georgia officials did not want the infectious diseases aboard slave ships to spread to Georgia's colonists. They built a special, nine-story station on Tybee Island, off the northeastern coast of Georgia. There, all slaves brought into the colony were **quarantined**, or kept away from others, until they could be examined by doctors. Slaves with diseases were kept on the island until they recovered or died. Those who died on the island were buried in unmarked graves.

Slaves on Georgia plantations lived in small houses called slave quarters.

TO BE SOLD, on WEDNESDAY 3d AUGUST next.
By COWPER & TELFAIRS,
A CARGO
Of 170 prime young likely healthy
GUINEA SLAVES,
Last imported, in the Bark Friends, William Ross Master, directly from Angola.   Savannah, July 25, 1774.

To be Sold at Private Sale, any Time before the 18th of next Month,

THE PLANTATION, containing one hundred acres, on which the subscriber lives, very pleasantly situated on Savannah River in sight of town.   The terms of sale may be known by applying to
July 21, 1774   RICHARD WYLLY.

WANTED,

AN OVERSEER thoroughly qualified to undertake the settlement of a River Swamp Plantation on the Alatamaha River.   Any such person, who can bring proper recommendations, may hear of great encouragement by applying to   NATHANIEL HALL.

THE subscriber being under an absolute necessity of closing his concerns without delay, gives this last publick notice, that all persons indebted to him by bond, note or otherwise, who do not discharge the same by the first day of October next, will find their respective obligations, &c in the hands of an Attorney to be sued for without distinction.   It is hoped those concerned will avail themselves of this notice.
                                        PHILIP BOX.

RUN AWAY the 20th of May last from John Forbes, Esq.'s plantation in St. John's parish, TWO NEGROES, named BILLY and QUAMINA, of the Guiney Country, and speak good English.   Billy is lusty and well made, about 5 feet 10 or 11 inches high, of a black complexion, has lost some of his upper teeth, and had on when he went away a white negroe cloth jacket and trowsers of the same. Quamina is stout and well made, about 5 feet 10 or 11 inches high, very black, has his country marks on his face, had on when he went away a jacket, trowsers, and robbin, of white negroe cloth.   Whoever takes up said Negroes, and deliver them to me at the above plantation, or to the Warden of the Work-House in Savannah, shall receive a reward of 20s. besides what the law allows.
                                        DAVIS AUSTIN.

Advertisements for slave auctions and runaway slaves were common in Georgia newspapers.

Humans or Property?

In Georgia, as in other colonies, slaves were treated as property instead of as human beings. Slaves had very few rights in Georgia. Their masters controlled every aspect of their lives.

Slaves who survived the boat trip to Georgia were cleaned up and prepared for auction. At a slave auction in Savannah, whole families of Africans might be put up for sale. But few family members were sold together. Most were split up and never saw their loved ones again.

Being sold at auction was a terrible experience. Each slave was paraded around and displayed like an animal. Sellers pointed out strong muscles, white teeth, and other good physical qualities. Then buyers began bidding against one another. The highest bidder became the slave's new owner.

A slave's treatment depended upon the slave's master. On some plantations, slaves were allowed to marry and live together. Other masters refused to recognize slave marriages. Whether married or unmarried, slaves could still be sold away from their families.

Slaves were punished for many different offenses. For example, slaves who refused to work or who did not work hard or fast enough were punished. They might be whipped or beaten with sticks.

Slave Laws

Other laws passed in Georgia about slaves included the following:

- Slaves had to have permits to leave their plantations.

- Slaves could not meet in large groups.

- Slaves could not drink beer or liquor at any time.

- Slaves could not be taught to read or write.

- Slaves could not play drums, blow on horns, or make any unusual noises.

For a slave, running away was considered a very serious crime. If they were caught, runaways were whipped, sold, or even killed. Despite this punishment, slaves were sometimes willing to take the risk. Slaves ran away in groups and alone. Many looked for safety in Georgia's swamps and wilderness. Others fled to Florida. Here, they formed their own communities, building homes, growing crops, and raising livestock. These runaway slaves became known as maroons.

Slaves had little hope that they or their children would ever be free. Children born to slave mothers in colonial Georgia were considered slaves themselves. It did not matter whether the fathers of the children were freemen or not.

There were a few laws in Georgia that gave slaves protection. For example, masters were required to feed, clothe, and shelter their slaves. The masters could be jailed or fined if they did not. Violent slave beatings were also outlawed in Georgia. However, white witnesses were needed to report cruel masters to the authorities. As a result, few masters were charged and convicted of cruelty.

Sold Away

One of the worst punishments that slaves endured was to be sold away from their families and friends. John Brown was the slave son of slave parents. He was sold away from his parents when he was just ten years old. He later described his feelings about the event:

Finney paid the money, and I was marched off. I looked round and saw my poor mother stretching out her hands after me. She ran up, and overtook us, but Finney, who was behind me, and between me and my mother, would not let her approach, though she begged and prayed to be allowed to kiss me for the last time, and bid me good bye. I was so stupefied with grief and fright, that I could not shed a tear, though my heart was bursting....That was the last time I ever saw her, nor do I know whether she is alive or dead at this hour.

Working on a Rice Plantation

Slaves were the backbone of Georgia's plantation economy. Most slaves in Georgia worked on the rice and indigo plantations in the coastal areas. They performed all the labor needed to care for the crops. People taken from West Africa also brought valuable rice farming knowledge with them.

Life was not easy for slaves on rice plantations. Working in the fields, slaves stood in muddy water up to their knees. The swampy rice fields were home to mosquitoes, poisonous snakes, and other creatures. Many slaves died of malaria and yellow fever. These were diseases carried by mosquitoes. Other slaves died of snakebites, pneumonia (a disease of the lungs), and sunstroke (an illness caused by spending too much time in the sun).

Slaves on rice plantations worked under the task system. Each slave was given a specific job to do. When the slaves finished their tasks, they reported to the overseer. The overseer was the person in charge of all the slaves. Those who finished early could go home and tend their own gardens. Those who worked slowly or did not finish could be punished.

Geechee Culture

Some of Georgia's slaves were able to preserve their culture better than others. The Geechee, living on rice plantations on Georgia's sea islands, were one such group. Kidnapped from West Africa's Rice Coast, the Geechee were prized by plantation owners for their knowledge of rice growing. Because of the isolated location of Georgia's island plantations, the Geechee managed to keep many of their customs and beliefs alive. They even created their own language, from African and English words.

Slave Life

Not all Georgia slaves worked in the fields. Some were taught such skills as carpentry or blacksmithing. Others worked as house slaves. House slaves served as maids, nannies, cooks, nurses, laundry workers, carriage drivers, or butlers.

Some slaves worked as household servants, avoiding the harsh labor of the fields.

Most slaves lived in tiny cabins. Some were no bigger than 12 feet (3.6 meters) by 12 feet. On some plantations, slave homes were built of sticks and poles covered over with clay or palmetto leaves. The homes had damp dirt floors and thin walls that let cold air in. Insects and rodents were common roommates for the slaves.

Slave families lived in small, poorly built cabins. They owned little or no furniture.

Slaves had little or no furniture. If a slave was lucky, there might be a bed to sleep on. Another slave might own only a blanket to wrap up in at night. Some slaves owned kettles or frying pans to cook in. Others carved their own plates or bowls from wood or other materials. For food, slaves were given a weekly supply of corn and allowed to keep whatever they grew in their own gardens. They were rarely given meat.

Slaves owned few clothes. Those that they did own were often frayed and tattered. Their shirts, trousers, and dresses were often old rags that had been sewn together. Any new clothes for slaves were made out of cheap cotton or wool. Few slaves wore shoes.

Slaves who became ill might have doctors called for them. But many sick slaves were on their own. As a result, slaves tried to develop their own medicines to heal themselves. They used plants, herbs, and roots to make healing potions. On a large plantation, an owner might build an infirmary, or hospital, for slaves. But slaves with cruel masters might be forced to work even when they were sick.

Despite these horrible conditions, most slaves kept their spirits up. They created songs to sing in the rice fields while they worked. On Saturday nights, they had parties and other gatherings, where they would play music, sing, and dance together. Slave musicians made their own instruments out of animal bones, skins, gourds, and horsehair.

Savannah would find its slave trade disrupted by the war the colonies would fight for their independence from England. Once the war ended, however, Georgia's slave trade started up again, stronger than before. Despite the efforts of some northern politicians, U.S. laws continued to protect Georgia's plantation economy.

Slaves on rice plantations worked long and hard. Here, they load the rice into barges to be shipped to market.

Slave Punishment

In an 1854 narrative, John Brown describes a slave's punishment.

This slave was punished for secretly marrying the slave of another master.

Slaves often suffered cruel punishments, such as being tied up or beaten.

*He was secured and brought back to quarters, and the other slaves were called together to witness the infliction upon him of a punishment called **bucking**. The poor fellow having been stripped stark naked, his hands were fast tied and brought down over his knees, he being compelled, for this purpose, to assume a sitting posture, with his knees doubled up under his chin. A stout stake was then thrust under [the backs of his thighs], so that he was rendered completely powerless. In this position he was turned first on one side then on the other, and flogged with willow switches and the cowhide.... It was two weeks before he went to work again.*

This is the Place to affix the STAMP.

Chapter Six

A State Divided

In the early 1700s, Great Britain began passing new laws that harmed Georgia's economy. These British laws restricted trade in the colonies. The laws also placed large taxes on goods that came to America from anywhere but Britain and its other colonies. One of the first laws that affected the colonies was the Molasses Act. Passed in 1733, the act put a heavy tax on any imported molasses, sugar, or rum.

In the 1760s, England passed even harsher acts. Great Britain needed money to pay off debts from the French and Indian War (1754–1763). In this war, the British had defeated the French after years of battle in the northern colonies and Canada. To raise money, British lawmakers passed the Sugar Act in 1764. Like the Molasses Act, the new act taxed sugar, molasses, and rum imported into the colonies.

A colonial newspaper makes fun of the Stamp Act, passed in 1765 by the British government.

Georgia residents were greatly angered by the Sugar Act. Merchants there made a lot of money by trading lumber for molasses in the Caribbean. A tax on molasses cut into the merchants' wealth.

In 1765, Great Britain passed the Stamp Act. This act was one of several laws that became known by the colonists as the Intolerable Acts. The Stamp Act placed a tax on newspapers and other printed materials, including letters, legal documents, pamphlets, and fliers. Colonists were required to purchase a special stamp for all such goods. This was the first tax that was placed directly on the colonists themselves, and not on foreign goods.

Another Intolerable Act forced colonists to house and feed British troops sent from England to keep the peace. The colonists had to do this at their own expense. The act even required colonists to provide the troops with "small beer, cider, or rum mixed with water."

Despite these new taxes, Georgians were slower to anger than most other colonists. Georgia still relied more heavily on Great Britain for economic help than other colonies did. In addition, the colony relied on British troops to protect its borders against the Creek and Cherokee. Finally, because the colony was so young, many of Georgia's settlers had been born in England. These colonists had greater loyalty to the king than others did.

Georgia's First Newspaper

In April 1763, Georgia's first newspaper, the *Georgia Gazette*, was published. At first, it seemed as if the weekly paper would have a very short life. In November 1765, publisher James Johnston had to stop printing his paper because he could not afford to pay the new tax imposed by the Stamp Act. Six months later, however, Johnston was able to begin publishing the *Gazette* again when the Stamp Act was repealed. The newspaper continued to be printed until early 1776.

For all these reasons, Georgia officials refused to take part in tax rebellions that were being held in other colonies. In 1765, Georgia was one of four colonies that did not send representatives to a special meeting in New York to protest the Stamp Act. The other colonies were angry with the newest colony. South Carolina threatened to stop trading with Georgia unless it actively supported rebellion. In Charleston, Patriots, or those opposed to English rule, stated that Georgia should be "amputated from the rest of their brethren, as a rotten part that might spread a dangerous infection."

Patriotism Swells

In 1765, many colonists in Georgia remained loyal to the king. But the number of Georgians who were unhappy with the British continued to grow. Many of those who supported the Patriots were the merchants and rich planters in the Low Country. These wealthy men were more affected than other Georgians by the taxes that Great Britain was imposing on the colonies.

As problems between colonists and the British grew, Sons of Liberty groups sprang up in Georgia. The Sons of Liberty were groups of Patriots that formed in all of the colonies. By the end of 1765, Savannah's Sons of Liberty group had grown strong and was ready for a fight. The Liberty Boys, as the group members were known, got their chance in December. That month, the first set of stamps arrived in Savannah from Great Britain.

First, the Liberty Boys threatened to burn down the warehouse holding the stamps. Then they carried a dummy representing Georgia's stamp officer through Savannah. The dummy was later hanged and burned. The frightened stamp officer escaped from the state. The stamps were sent back to England unsold.

Many Patriot leaders tried to convince Georgia colonists to support their cause.

Georgia Stands Alone

Although support for the Patriot cause continued to grow in Georgia, the colony was not yet ready to cut off ties with England. In the fall of 1774, Georgia was the only colony that did not send delegates to the First Continental Congress. The congress was a meeting to decide what actions should be taken against England. It was held in Philadelphia, Pennsylvania.

At the meeting, the congress agreed not to import or export goods to Great Britain. The colonies also passed a Declaration of Rights and Grievances, which was sent to the king in England. The declaration told the king what the colonies thought about the Intolerable Acts.

In January 1775, a number of important Georgia colonists attended the first meeting of what they called the Provincial Congress. Provincial congresses were law-making bodies that were formed by Patriots in many colonies. Some people at the meeting hoped that their new congress would replace Georgia's royal government, headed by James Wright. For now, however, the majority of Georgia Patriots were afraid to cut off economic ties with their mother country.

Tondee's Tavern

In the 1770s, the Patriot movement in Georgia grew ever stronger. As events between England and the colonies heated up, more Georgians sided with the Patriots. Now, the Patriots needed a safe place to meet and discuss these events. Tondee's Tavern in Savannah became the headquarters for Georgia's Patriot movement.

Tondee's Tavern was the meeting place for Savannah's Sons of Liberty group.

Tondee's Tavern was founded in Savannah in 1766 by Swiss immigrant Peter Tondee. The tavern was the most popular spot in town. Here, colonists could get a warm meal, have a mug of beer, and learn all the local gossip.

In 1774, delegates from each parish met at the tavern to discuss how Georgia should react to British taxes. During one meeting, Peter Tondee guarded the door. He made sure that only people on a special list got inside. At this meeting, the Patriots set up a committee to communicate with the other colonies. This type of committee was called a "committee of correspondence."

In late 1774, more than a hundred men from all of the colony's parishes met at Tondee's Tavern. Together, they created the framework of Georgia's first state government. At the same meeting, delegates were elected to represent Georgia at the Second Continental Congress.

At the 1774 meeting, a Council of Safety was set up. The mission of the council was to hunt down Loyalists, or Tories. These were people who were still loyal to the British. The council also wanted to seize British weapons and gunpowder and control Georgia's military. By the end of 1775, the Council of Safety was firmly in control of the colony (although the royal governor, James Wright, still considered himself in charge). The first leader of the council was Button Gwinnett. Gwinnett would be one of the three men from Georgia to sign the Declaration of Independence.

The battle of Lexington in 1775 touched off the Revolutionary War.

The Declaration of Independence, written in 1776, was a document that proclaimed the freedom of the thirteen colonies from Great Britain. But now, Gwinnett needed to prepare his colony for war.

War Begins

In April 1775, war broke out between the colonies and Great Britain. It was called the Revolutionary War. The colonists were fighting for independence from England. The war began with the Battles of Lexington and Concord in Massachusetts. The battles enraged many people in Georgia. The thought of Americans being killed by British troops caused many Georgians to begin supporting the Patriots.

After the battles, the Sons of Liberty in Savannah raided an ammunition storage building. Legend says that ammunition, rice, and money were sent to Massachusetts to help its fight against the British. In June, Patriots disrupted the celebration of the king's birthday. They marched through Savannah's streets carrying their guns and bayonets (sharp blades attached to the barrel of muskets or rifles).

Georgians were still deeply divided, however. When the Second Continental Congress was held in May 1775, Georgia was again absent. The three Georgians who had been chosen to attend decided not to go. They felt that they did not represent the majority of Georgians.

The other twelve colonies resented Georgia's absence from the Second Continental Congress. At the congress, delegates from the other colonies voted to stop trading with Georgia. Again, Georgia's closest neighbor was one of the angriest. South Carolina officials said that Georgians were "unworthy of the rights of freemen." Some South Carolina delegates even threatened to invade Georgia if the British spilled any more American blood on American soil. The threat showed that South Carolina would no longer tolerate Georgia's lukewarm support of the Patriots.

In June 1775, Georgia Patriots marched through the streets with guns and bayonets to "celebrate" the king's birthday.

A Colony Divided

In Georgia, the Revolutionary War divided friends, families, and neighbors. Fathers watched with sadness as their sons took up arms against the British. Friends who had once helped each other were now enemies.

At the beginning of the war, Loyalists had to carefully watch their words and actions, especially in Savannah. Merchants who did not follow the bans on English trade might find that they no longer had any customers. Some were ordered to leave the colony. Others suffered a worse fate. They were tarred and feathered. Tarring and feathering was a colonial punishment in which hot tar was poured over a person's body, which was then covered with feathers.

One Loyalist who was punished by the Savannah Patriots was John Hopkins, a seaman. Hopkins was drinking at a Savannah tavern in July 1775. He made the mistake of proposing an anti-Patriot toast: "Damnation to America." The next day, Hopkins was tarred and feathered. To escape being hanged from Savannah's Liberty Tree, he was forced to propose the following toast: "Damnation to all Tories and success to American liberty." (Liberty Trees were designated meeting spots for Patriots to discuss the actions of Great Britain.)

A Cruel and Unusual Punishment

Tarring and feathering was an awful punishment. The mere threat of it was enough to cause some Tories to become Patriots. The pain and suffering of a person who was tarred and feathered continued long after the act was over. Removing tar from the body often resulted in the peeling away of layers of skin. This could result in infection, illness, and death.

The Prohibitory Act, passed in December 1775, broke off all British trade with the colonies. It also allowed those loyal to the British to take away ships owned by Patriots. Many people who had been undecided or who had favored the British changed their minds after the act was passed.

CHAPTER SEVEN

The Fight for Freedom

In the spring and summer of 1775, Georgia colonists struck some of their first blows for freedom. In May, Patriots in Savannah took control of the town's armory, the place where weapons and ammunition were stored. They removed about 600 pounds (270 kilograms) of gunpowder from the building, which they sent to the Continental (Patriot) army.

Two months later, Georgia captain Oliver Bowen and several South Carolina captains seized a British ship off Tybee Island. The ship was loaded with 9,000 pounds (4,040 kilograms) of gunpowder for British troops in the colonies. More than half of the gunpowder was sent to the Continental army. In September, a second British boat filled with powder was seized off Georgia's coast.

Off the coast of Savannah, Georgia colonists seized ships packed with gunpowder and ammunition meant for British troops.

The British Plan

The conflicts of 1775 were not the only wartime actions in Georgia. Early in the war, British commanders had created a plan to take control of the southern colonies. They would start by conquering Georgia, the youngest and weakest colony.

There were a number of reasons for starting in Georgia. First, Georgia had more Loyalists than most other colonies. Further, Georgia was not very well defended. Georgia also had a large population of slaves who might fight for the British. Finally, Georgia had several Native American tribes that might join the British forces.

Once they had taken Georgia, the British expected to continue north through the Carolinas to Virginia. Even if they could not conquer the other twelve colonies, the British believed that they could keep control of Georgia. Most British officers thought that Georgia would remain a British colony, no matter what happened in the north.

Until early 1776, the royal governor, James Wright, remained in Georgia, still acting as the representative of King George III. Until the problems with England, Wright had been widely respected by most of Georgia's colonists. He had helped bring prosperity to the struggling colony.

In early 1776, Georgia's royal governor, James Wright, escaped to the British ships anchored off Tybee Island.

In January 1776, three British ships anchored off Tybee Island. Responding to the threat, the Council of Safety ordered that Wright be arrested. Georgia's royal governor realized that the colony was no longer safe for him. He fled to the British warships waiting off the coast.

With Wright gone, the Patriots were now in complete control of Georgia's government. In April, the Provincial Congress adopted a document called the Rules and Regulations to govern themselves. This document, which outlined the new government, is considered Georgia's first constitution. A constitution is a document that sets out the guiding principles of a state or nation. Archibald Bulloch, a former member of the Lower House, was the first leader, or president. Savannah would serve as the colonial capital.

In the summer of 1776, the Second Continental Congress approved the Declaration of Independence. In August, Georgia's delegates signed the important document. The Declaration severed the thirteen colonies' relationship with Great Britain and created the United States of America. By signing, Georgia showed that it would stand with the rest of the colonies against Great Britain.

Signing the Declaration of Independence smoothed out Georgia's relations with the other colonies, especially South Carolina. Georgia was soon supporting the war efforts in that state. It sent more gunpowder to the north. The Continental Congress welcomed Georgia back into the fold by ordering a battalion to be raised to defend it.

The Fighting Begins

The first Revolutionary battle on Georgia soil occurred in the late winter of 1776. The conflict is known as the Battle of the Rice Boats. On March 2, British troops sailed up the Savannah River. They captured Georgia boats loaded with rice. The British planned to use the rice to feed hungry troops. The following day, 500 Patriots from Georgia and another 100 from South Carolina took action. The rebels set a ship on fire and cut it loose. The burning ship floated into the captured rice boats. It destroyed the boats and the rice.

Georgia Patriots fought to capture Florida from British control.

Georgia Patriots and soldiers fought in battles in other areas. Until 1778, for example, they often took part in attacks upon neighboring Florida, now a British territory. Spain had lost Florida to Great Britain after siding against the British in the French and Indian War. During the Revolution, the region had become a safe place for colonists loyal to the British. The Patriots hoped to defeat British troops stationed at Saint Augustine and take control of Florida.

The city of Savannah was captured by the British during a bloody battle in December 1778.

From August 1776 to July 1778, the Patriots attempted three separate attacks against British Florida. During that time, they built forts to protect the main route from Georgia to Florida. However, all three attacks failed. Heat, lack of food, and disease all played a part in the failures. The Georgians also had to deal with attacks by Creek tribes fighting on the side of the British. Further, there were Loyalist spies within the Continental troops.

Georgia Captured

Savannah was the largest settlement in Georgia. But it was still small compared to other colonial cities. By the end of 1778, there were only about 450 houses there. As the capital of Georgia's new government, however, Savannah was the heart of Georgia.

In July 1778, Georgia was one of eleven colonies to sign the Articles of Confederation. These articles served as the first constitution of the United States of America. Five months later, the British attacked and captured Savannah. The Patriots defending the capital were outnumbered and outgunned by the British troops. During the battle for Savannah, about 300 Georgians were killed. Later, British commander Archibald Campbell reported: "The capital of Georgia, the shipping in the harbour, with a large quantity of provisions, fell into our possession before it was dark, without any loss on our side than [one officer]."

The British were now determined to take control of all of Georgia. In January 1779, they began a march into the state. Town after town fell to the British. Citizens in the captured towns were forced to swear loyalty to King George. Those who refused were treated roughly. Patriots' homes were burned, and their crops were destroyed. Colonists who were outspoken against the British were shot or hanged.

By July 1779, James Wright felt that it was safe to return to Savannah as the royal governor. One of his first actions was to cancel laws that had been passed by the Patriot government in Georgia. Wright would remain the governor of a captured Georgia until 1782. Georgia was the only colony that had a government run by Loyalists during the Revolutionary War.

The Loyalists were now in control. But the American government did not give up. After the fall of Savannah, the Patriots fled to Augusta. When Augusta fell soon afterward, they moved to Heard's Fort in Wilkes County, Georgia.

Surprise Attacks

With Georgia under British control, many Patriots fled to safety in the north. Some joined Continental troops in the Carolinas to fight the British there. Other Patriots chose to remain in Georgia. Here, they used guerrilla warfare against their enemies. Guerrilla warfare is a type of fighting in which small groups of fighters carry out surprise attacks on an enemy.

Rebels in Georgia used surprise attacks to fight the British.

Many Georgians joined guerrilla groups that roamed the countryside in search of Loyalist soldiers. Others raided English plantations along the border between Georgia and Florida. Some Patriots even became pirates, attacking boats carrying Florida Loyalists. They also raided rice boats to prevent the food from supplying British soldiers.

One Georgian who joined the guerrillas was John Dooly. Dooly organized and commanded a group of soldiers to patrol Georgia's backcountry. In early 1779, Dooly led an attack on 700 Loyalist troops in Wilkes County. Many were killed or captured.

Another Georgia Patriot was Elijah Clarke. He was a poor, uneducated backcountry settler. Clarke fought against hostile Cherokee and Creek warriors during the war. When Georgia was in enemy hands, he moved up to the Carolinas and took part in guerrilla raids.

Mordecai Sheftall also played an important role in fighting the British. Sheftall was the son of a Jewish settler who had come to Savannah in 1733. Sheftall was a wealthy, well-respected Savannah merchant. He was captured in 1778 while fighting to keep the British from capturing Savannah. Some of the Patriots who were defending the city swam across the Savannah River and escaped. But Sheftall's fifteen-year-old son was with him. The boy could not swim and Sheftall refused to leave his son behind.

The Volunteers of Augusta

Songs about the fighting in Georgia were written by both Patriot and Loyalist troops.

The following Loyalist song was written after the Patriots took back Augusta from the British.

The rebels they murder,—Revenge is the word,
Let each lad return with blood on his sword;
See [the colonel's] pale ghost point afresh to his wound;
We'll conquer, my boys, or fall dead to the ground.
Then brandish your swords, and constantly sing,
Success to our Troops, our Country, and King.

As a prisoner of war, Sheftall was starved and treated badly by the British. However, he refused to tell the enemy where the Patriots stored their weapons. Sheftall later escaped and rejoined the Continental army. Over the course of the war, he was promoted, becoming the highest-ranking Jewish officer in the Continental army. He even had his own regiment, which he outfitted with his own money.

Loyalist raiders were also active in Georgia during the war. A group known as the Florida Rangers attacked Patriot homes and stole cattle along the Georgia border. One leader of the rangers was Thomas Brown. Brown was from Georgia. He had a burning hatred of the Patriots. In 1775, he had been tarred and feathered by Augusta's

Sons of Liberty. His injuries were so severe that he could not walk for six months.

In 1779, Brown helped the British defend Savannah. The following year, he was given control of Augusta, his hometown. Here, Brown took his revenge on the Patriots. He raided their homes and settlements, took their property, and had them hanged.

Nancy Morgan Hart: Fact or Fiction?

According to legend, Nancy Morgan Hart was a tough Georgia frontier woman. She supported the cause of colonial freedom. Some stories describe her as tall, red-haired, and cross-eyed. Tales tell that Hart's home was invaded by six Loyalists looking for a hot meal. While cooking, Hart offered the men plenty of homemade whiskey.

After the Loyalists were drunk, Hart carefully stole their guns from them. By the time the men realized what she was doing, it was too late. Hart killed one of the Loyalists, wounded another, and held the rest hostage until her daughter returned with help. The remaining Loyalists were hanged. Whether fact or fiction, Nancy Morgan Hart was honored in 1853, when the state of Georgia named Hart County after her.

Slavery During the War

At the beginning of the war, there were about 5,000 blacks in Georgia. Most were slaves. The war greatly affected slaves in Georgia.

Many slaves believed that if Great Britain won the war, they would be freed. The British encouraged this idea. They wanted slaves to revolt against their Patriot masters. Early in the war, for example, Virginia's royal governor issued a special decree declaring that any slave who wished to fight for Britain would be freed. The proclamation brought hope to many slaves who had thought they would never be free. As a result, slaves in Georgia and other southern colonies began to rebel against their masters. Some escaped into the swamps of Georgia and to Florida. Others fled to the British, seeking shelter and freedom.

By early 1776, a number of Georgia slaves had fled to Tybee Island. Their Patriot owners were furious. One Georgia Patriot stated, "It is far better for the public and the owners, if the deserted negroes…who are on Tybee Island, be shot, if they cannot be taken." On March 25, forty Patriots, aided by thirty Creek, attacked these slaves. Florida's governor later wrote that the raid was "savage barbarity." The slaves were captured.

Although the British had promised freedom, they, too, generally viewed the slaves as property. Throughout the war, Georgia slaves were taken as "war booty" by the Loyalists. The captured slaves were sometimes given to Loyalist soldiers in payment for their service. Other slaves were sold or traded at will. Many were shipped to the Caribbean. Some were recaptured by Patriot raiders. Many slaves died during the raids or the forced marches from one region to another.

Unlike other colonies, Georgia and South Carolina refused to allow their slaves to fight in return for freedom. Slave owners feared what would happen if their slaves were given weapons. In 1779, the Continental Congress urged both southern colonies to create a black regiment with 3,000 slaves. Georgia's Patriot leaders refused.

The British did not give weapons to all the slaves who came to them. When Savannah was under British control, slaves from nearby plantations were usually forced to perform manual labor. Manual labor is hard work that is done with the hands. Some slaves, however, were allowed to bear weapons and fight for the British.

When the British eventually **evacuated** Savannah, they took some slaves with them, but not as free blacks. Ten families that sailed to Jamaica took more than 1,500 slaves with them. Another man fled to the Caribbean with 170 slaves to put them to work on his plantations there.

The King of England's Soldiers

Some slaves who had trained as British soldiers were not willing to give up their newfound freedom. They fled into the swamps along the Savannah River. Here, they built twenty-one homes and planted crops. They surrounded their new settlement with a 4-foot-high (1.2-meter) wall. These former slaves called themselves the King of England's Soldiers. They raided plantations and attacked state troops. They remained free and undefeated until 1787. That year, Georgia's government sent troops into the swamps to capture the former slaves and destroy their settlements. While some were taken prisoner, others fled to the swamps of South Carolina.

Native Involvement

In addition to rebellious slaves, Georgia colonists worried about which side the native tribes in the region would support. Early in the war, colonists offered gifts of rum to the Creek Indians. The gifts were supposed to persuade the Creek to remain **neutral.** Despite the gifts, some Creek sided with the British. They saw the chance to preserve what was left of their shrinking territory in Georgia. The Creek who sided with the British even united with the Choctaw, an enemy tribe, to fight against the colonists.

The Cherokee were also divided. At first, the young warriors sided with the British. Like the Creek, the Cherokee saw their land being taken by Georgia's white settlers. Cherokee warriors began raiding colonial settlements. They were the first Native Americans in Georgia to openly attack the Patriots.

The Patriots responded to the Native American attacks by burning and destroying many Cherokee settlements. The colonists, in the words of a South Carolina official, were to "cut up every Indian corn-field, and burn every Indian town—and…every Indian taken shall be the slave and property of the taker." Tribal members were either killed or sold into slavery.

In May 1777, the Cherokee signed a treaty with Georgia and South Carolina. As a result, the tribe surrendered thousands of acres of land. Still, some young warriors refused to give up. They split from the Cherokee, forming their own tribe, known as the Chickamauga. The British encouraged the Chickamauga to keep fighting the colonists. The British gave the warriors weapons and other items. Even after the war ended in British defeat, the Chickamauga would continue to fight settlers in the south.

The Battle of Kettle Creek

In early 1779, the struggle for independence was going badly for Georgia's Patriots. They had suffered defeat after defeat. Many settlements had been captured by British troops. The Patriots needed a victory.

In 1779, British soldiers won most battles against Georgia's militia.

In February, the Patriots got their wish at the Battle of Kettle Creek. About 350 American soldiers from Georgia and South Carolina attacked Loyalist soldiers from the Carolinas. The Loyalists had camped out at Kettle Creek in Wilkes County, Georgia.

The Patriots surprised the Loyalists and killed their commander. The rest of the Loyalists panicked and fled.

The Battle of Kettle Creek was a turning point in the war. It gave Continental troops hope that they could win the war against England.

During the battle, about twenty Loyalists were killed. Another twenty were taken prisoner. Others decided to give up and go home after the battle.

The battle was a surprise defeat to the British in the south. More importantly, it gave the Continental army a much-needed boost. At this time, the Patriot troops were being beaten everywhere. Kettle Creek gave the Americans confidence that the British could really be defeated. Further, any Loyalists who might have joined the British army in the south now thought twice about doing so.

Recapturing the Colony

Almost as soon as Savannah was captured, Georgia Patriots began planning to take the town back. In September 1779, colonial troops, under the command of Major General Benjamin Lincoln, tried to recapture the city. They were assisted by about 4,000 French troops under the command of Count Charles-Henri d'Estaing. The French had joined the war as **allies** with the Americans. D'Estaing brought twenty-two French ships from the Caribbean to help free Georgia's capital from the British.

The siege of Savannah lasted for more than a month. The worst day of fighting took place on October 9. On that day, more than 1,000 American and French soldiers were killed. It was one of the bloodiest battles of the war.

Casimir Pulaski

Although born in Poland, Count Casimir Pulaski was dedicated to the cause of American liberty. After arriving in the United States in 1777, Pulaski sent a letter to General George Washington. He wrote that he "came here, where freedom is being defended, to serve it, and to live and die for it." Over the coming months, the Polish war hero would prove his commitment to freedom again and again.

Pulaski acted as a military adviser. He trained American officers in battle tactics. He even raised his own legion of cavalry, or soldiers who fought on horseback. The cavalry unit was made up of American, French, Polish, Irish, and German soldiers. General Pulaski was wounded on October 9 at the siege of Savannah. He died two days later.

The colonists were defeated at Savannah. But they were not ready to give up the fight to recapture Georgia. In April 1781, Continental troops began attacking Augusta. By early June, they had driven the British out of the town and out of that part of Georgia. Retreating British troops fled to Savannah.

In October 1781, the British commander, Lord Charles Cornwallis, surrendered at Yorktown, Virginia. His army had been defeated by General George Washington, commander of the Continental army. The event marked the last big battle of the Revolutionary War and victory for the United States. In the spring of 1782, British troops were ordered to evacuate Savannah.

By mid-July, the last British troops had left Savannah. On their way out of the city, the British took thousands of Loyalists and slaves with them. The Loyalists and slaves moved to such places as Nova Scotia in Canada, Florida, and the Bahamas. Now Georgia's Patriots could return home and begin the process of rebuilding their state.

GEORGIA.

HOUSE of ASSEMBLY, 15th July, 1783.

ORDERED, THAT his Honour the Governor and Council be recommended and requested to transmit to the Executive and Legislative Powers or Departments, in every State in the United States, a List of Persons at this Time within our Act of Attainder, Banishment, and Confiscation, and request a List from them of Persons named in their Law; so that, by this Correspondence, each State may know, or be informed from Time to Time, what is done by each State relative to those Persons so proscribed.

Extract from the Minutes,

(Signed) JOHN WILKINSON, Clk. G. A.

In COUNCIL, Savannah, 19th August, 1783.

PURSUANT to the foregoing Order of the Honourable the House of Assembly, passed at Augusta on the 15th July last past, the following Persons are named within our Act of Attainder, Banishment, and Confiscation, and stood proscribed on that Day.

By Order of his Honour the Governor in Council,

D. REES, Sec'y. Ex. Council.

A LIST of Persons on the Bill of Attainder, Banishment, and Confiscation, passed at Augusta, in the State of Georgia, on the Fourth Day of May, which was in the Year of our Lord One Thousand Seven Hundred and Eighty-Two, and of our Sovereignty and Independence the Sixth; to wit:

SIR James Wright, Bart.	George Kincaid	John Proctor	William Young
John Graham	William Knox	Daniel M'Girt	Matthew Moore
Alexander Wright	John Murray	James M'Girt	Henry Sharp
Lachlan M'Gillivray	George Cuthbert	George Aarons	Cordy Sharp
John Mullryne	William M'Gillivray	William Willis	William M'Natt
Josiah Tattnall	Peter Dean	Absalom Mincey	Samuel Montgomery
Basil Cowper	George Fox	Henry Cooper sen.	Benjamin Brantley
William Telfair	Moses Kirkland	Henry Cooper jun.	Elias Bonnel
Alexander M'Goun	John Lightenstone	William Cooper	Absalom Wells
Thomas Tallemach	William Lyford	Philip Dell	John Ferguson
Samuel Douglass	Andrew Hewat	James Dell	William Ried
Lewis Johnston sen.	Alexander Inglis	James Pace sen.	Thomas Beatty
Lewis Johnston jun.	James Brisbane	Christopher Fred. Triebner	Thomas Waters
William Johnston	William Miller	Stephen Dampier	Henry Williams
Samuel Farley	William Moss	Peter Blyth	John Douglass
James Alexander	Philip Moore	John Blyth	William White
James Butler	William Panton	Ulrick Gruber	Samuel Williams
John Wood	Thomas Skinner	Joseph Johnston	Daniel Philips
Robert Reid	John Mullryne Tattnall	John Johnston	James Gordon
John Storr	Charles William Mackinen	William Love	Abraham Wilkins
Thomas Ried	Alexander Rose	John Love	Samuel Wilkins
Philip Delegall sen.	Charles Wright sen.	John Thomas	Jonathan Wilkins
Philip Delegall jun.	Robert Porteous	David Russel	William Tidwell
John Glen	Jermyn Wright	Matthew Lyle	Reuben Sherral
John Bond Randell	Charles Wright (son of James)	Robert Miller	James Grierson (Colonel)
John Charles Lucena		John Roberson	Andrew Moore
Nathaniel Hall	John M'Gillivray	Daniel Howel	John Howard
Thomas Gibbons	Timothy Barnard	Alexander Carter	William Manson
John Fox jun.	Isaac Delyon	Robert Wolfington	James Ingram
John Simpson of Sabine Fields	Peter Edwards	Willoughby Tucker	Edward Alhton
Matthew Stewart	Roger Kelsall	John M'Cormick	James Seymour (Rev.)
Thomas Ross	Thomas Young	Paul M'Cormick	Martin Weatherford
John Joachim Zubly	Simon Munro	Robert Henderson	John Henderson
David Zubly jun.	Henry Munro	Lud Mobley	John Weatherford
	James Spalding	James Herbert	

CHAPTER EIGHT

Statehood

❀❀❀❀❀❀❀❀❀❀❀❀❀❀❀❀❀❀❀❀❀❀❀❀❀❀❀❀

The war was over and the British were leaving. The Patriots moved their government from Augusta back to Savannah. They held their first postwar meeting in the capital just two days after the last British soldier had left. Soon, Georgians began returning from the north, where many had taken shelter.

People who returned to Georgia after the war found destruction everywhere. Plantations had been destroyed. Homes had been burned. Crops had been ruined. In addition, plantation owners found that most of their slaves had fled or left with the British.

After the war, Loyalists who tried to remain in Georgia were punished. About 340 men who had been active for the British during the war were banned from Georgia forever. The state also took their property. One of these men was James Wright, the former royal governor. Officials also

After the war, Georgia lawmakers published lists of Loyalists who were banned from entering the state. The Loyalists also had their land taken from them.

asked for lists of Loyalists from other colonies in order to prevent them from settling in Georgia.

Eventually, some Loyalists were allowed to return to their homes. At first, they were harassed by their neighbors. Over the years, however, the hard feelings faded away. Life returned to normal.

Black Americans played an important role in rebuilding Georgia after the Revolutionary War. Most black Americans in Georgia were slaves.

Repairing the Economy

Before the war, Georgia had been the poorest and least populated of the colonies. After the war, the state was in worse shape than before. Georgia's economy had been ruined. But many Georgians were hopeful about their future. In 1782, Governor John Martin wrote, "It is true this war has made us poor, and we are not ashamed to own it; because our cause is just; but we shall soon be rich and happy."

Slowly, state businesses began to recover. Skilled tradesmen from up north moved into the state, searching for better job opportunities. Many set up shops in Savannah and Augusta. Black Americans also played a major role in Georgia's recovery. Blacks, both slave and free, worked in city shops and factories and at coastal docks. They also helped build Georgia's roads and bridges.

As they considered the future, Georgia's officials realized that their state could not thrive on its own. They knew that it would be better off as part of the new United States of America. On January 2, 1788, Georgia officials ratified, or approved, the new U.S. Constitution. The Constitution, created at the Constitutional Convention in the summer of 1787, laid out the rules for the new federal government. Georgia was the fourth state to join the new nation.

Return to the Plantation System

After the war, there was demand for Georgia rice in Great Britain and British colonies. This demand guaranteed that the plantation system would grow again. By 1785, the plantation system was once again the basis of Georgia's economy. Georgia merchants firmly supported the plantation masters' right to own slaves. One merchant said that slavery was "to the Trade of the Country, as the Soul [is] to the Body." By 1790, there were about 30,000 blacks in the state. All but about 1,000 were slaves.

In 1793, Eli Whitney invented the cotton gin at a Savannah plantation. The cotton gin was a machine that could remove seeds from cotton fiber. The new invention could clean as much cotton in one day as a slave could clean in a year. Thanks to Whitney's new machine, cotton could now be produced in huge quantities and still cleaned quickly.

Whitney's new machine caused the demand for slaves to increase. As farmers planted more cotton, they needed more slaves to work in the fields. Slaves had to plant, tend, and pick the cotton before it could be sent through a cotton gin.

Cotton soon became the top crop in Georgia. Before long, the state's economy would become dependent upon cotton and the slaves needed to produce it.

In the years after the Revolution, raising cotton became Georgia's main industry. The demand for slaves to work in cotton fields soared.

In 1790, before the cotton boom, Georgia had about 29,000 slaves. By 1810, that number had skyrocketed to more than 105,000.

The University of Georgia

In 1785, Georgia became the first state to charter a state-supported university, the University of Georgia. Six years later, a 630-acre (252-hectare) parcel of land on the Oconee River was chosen as the site of the new college. At first, the university offered courses in classical studies, such as Greek and Latin. Later, it expanded its course selection to include law, agriculture, and mechanical studies. The university's first class graduated in 1804.

The president's house on the University of Georgia's campus looks like a wealthy southern plantation owner's home.

Changes in the Wind

In the coming years, life in Georgia would change rapidly. The state's borders were redrawn, causing the state to shrink in size. Georgia's native population also shrank as Creek and Cherokee were driven from all their lands. By 1840, nearly all the native people of Georgia had been forced to move to the Indian Territory, now known as Oklahoma.

Although the native population plummeted after the war, the population of white Americans grew. Settlers flooded into the area, attracted by open land. The state used the lottery system to hand out the land. Parcels were first divided into lots of 200 acres (80 hectares). Then Georgia citizens had the chance to draw tickets and win the land. Heads of families were given two chances to win.

During the earliest years of the nineteenth century, Georgia's population boomed. Settlers flooded into the area, attracted by open land. Between 1790 and 1810, the state's population more than tripled, topping 250,000.

In the years to come, Georgia would play an important role in U.S. history. In the early 1800s, more and more people spoke out against slavery, especially in the northern states. Eventually, slavery, and Georgia's right to continue the practice, would cause the state to follow its southern neighbors and split from the rest of the United States. This split would lead to the Civil War (1861–1865), one of the darkest times in American history. Although the state recovered slowly from the war, today Georgia is one of the fastest-growing states in the nation.

Recipe
for a Tansey
[Spinach Omelette]

In colonial times, most households did not have printed cookbooks because they were too expensive. Instead, the mistress of the household would copy down her mother's recipes when she got married and established her own home. One popular dish handed down to many young women was Tansey or spinach omelette. This recipe was first written by Isabella Morris Ashfield (1705–1741) and passed down through her family.

Modern Version

6 eggs

1/2 cup heavy cream

1/2 cup spinach, cooked, drained, and chopped or 1/2 package frozen spinach, thawed

1/4 teaspoon nutmeg

1/4 teaspoon salt

2 tablespoons butter

1 orange, quartered

- Beat the eggs and cream together lightly with a fork.

- Stir in the spinach, nutmeg, and salt.

- Melt the butter in an omelette pan or heavy skillet over high heat. When the foam goes down, pour in the egg mixture.

- Reduce the heat and tilt the pan until the eggs are set. The pan may be covered to help set the omelette top.

- Fold the omelette in half and slide it onto a heated serving dish. Garnish with orange quarters. Serves 2.

This activity should be done with adult supervision.

Activity
Silhouette Art

Silhouettes were also called shades or shadows. The first silhouettes were painted images of a subject's shadow. These images were painted with lamp black, or soot, and reduced to fit in a small frame. This art form was popular in the colonies because people wanted portraits of their family members. Cameras were not yet invented.

Directions

*large sheet of black construction paper
small lamp • tape • chair
white crayon or white chalk
construction paper*

• This project requires two people, a model and someone to trace the shadow.

• Place the chair parallel to or in front of a wall. The model sits in the chair.

• The second person shines the light directly on the model. The model's profile should appear on the wall. Move the light source until the profiled shadow looks good.

• Tape the black paper on the wall to cover the model's profiled shadow.

• Carefully trace the outline of the model's head with the white chalk or crayon.

• Cut out the silhouette and paste it to another sheet of construction paper. Repeat the process by having the two participants change places.

This activity should be done with adult supervision.

GEORGIA
Time Line

1733
James Oglethorpe founds Savannah, the first permanent settlement in Georgia.

1742
The Battle of Bloody Marsh ends Spanish claims in Georgia.

1525
The Spanish found a settlement in Georgia.

| 1525 | 1550 | 1700 | 1725 |

1539
Hernando de Soto begins the expedition that will take him into Georgia.

1735
Augusta is founded by James Oglethorpe.

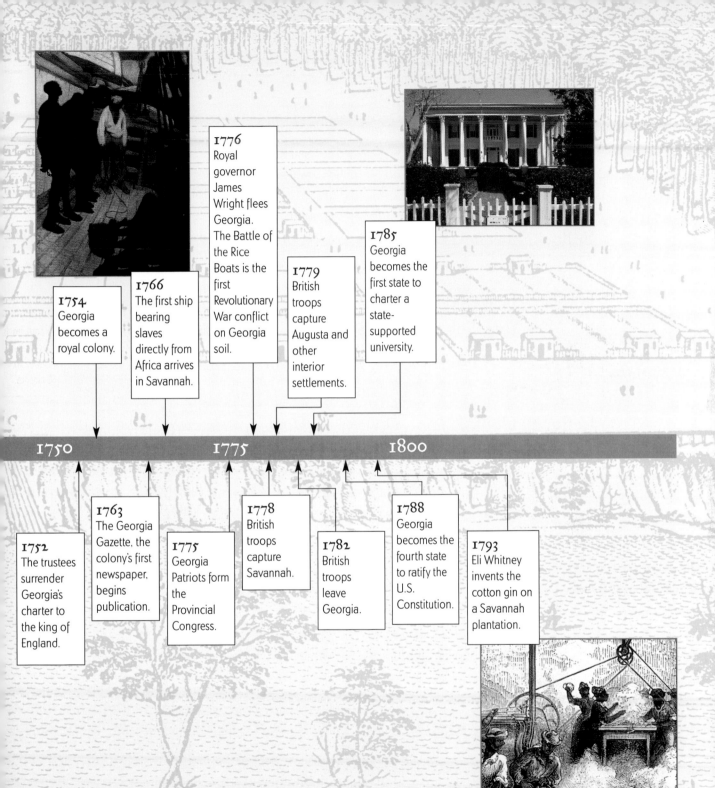

1776
Royal governor James Wright flees Georgia. The Battle of the Rice Boats is the first Revolutionary War conflict on Georgia soil.

1766
The first ship bearing slaves directly from Africa arrives in Savannah.

1754
Georgia becomes a royal colony.

1779
British troops capture Augusta and other interior settlements.

1785
Georgia becomes the first state to charter a state-supported university.

1750

1775

1800

1752
The trustees surrender Georgia's charter to the king of England.

1763
The Georgia Gazette, the colony's first newspaper, begins publication.

1775
Georgia Patriots form the Provincial Congress.

1778
British troops capture Savannah.

1782
British troops leave Georgia.

1788
Georgia becomes the fourth state to ratify the U.S. Constitution.

1793
Eli Whitney invents the cotton gin on a Savannah plantation.

Further Reading

Bullock, Steven C. *The American Revolution: A History in Documents.* New York: Oxford University Press, 2003.

Furbee, Mary Rodd. *Outrageous Women of Colonial America.* New York: John Wiley, 2001.

Hakim, Joy. *A History of US: Making Thirteen Colonies.* New York: Oxford University Press, 2002.

Lommel, Cookie. *James Oglethorpe: Humanitarian and Soldier.* Philadelphia: Chelsea House, 2001.

Wood, Peter H. *Strange New Land: Africans in Colonial America.* New York: Oxford University Press, 2003.

Glossary

allies those who help each other during times of war or hardship

apprentice a person who works for a tradesman in order to learn a trade

bluff a high, steep cliff

bucking a punishment in which a slave was tied and beaten

buffer something that separates two enemies

charter a document, issued by a ruler or government, granting rights and privileges

decline to grow smaller

epidemic the rapid spread of a disease that affects many people at one time

evacuate to withdraw from an area

export to ship goods for sale out of a port

hold the area below a ship's deck where cargo is stored

mechanics work involving machines and tools

neutral not taking part on either side during a war

palisade a fence made of wooden stakes

Parliament England's lawmaking body

plummet to drop quickly

quarantine to separate a person from others to prevent the spread of disease

shingles thin pieces of wood used to cover roofs and walls on the outsides of buildings

trustee a person who safeguards the property and affairs of a company or another person

ward a section of a town

wharf a landing place or pier where ships tie up and are loaded and unloaded

Index